# Never Alone

Leslie Tracey

**Never Alone**

Copyright © 2016 by Leslie Tracey
Published by T.N.T. Publishing
Oakdale, Louisiana 71463
www.courtneyartiste.com

**All Rights Reserved.** No part of this book may be reproduced, stored in a retrieval system, or transmitted in any form or by any means-electronic, mechanical, digital, photocopy, recording, or any other –except the brief quotations in printed reviews, without the prior written permission from Leslie Tracey/TNT Publishing, P.O. Box 16 Oakdale, LA 71463

ISBN-13: 978-0692691083

ISBN-10: 0692691081

All scripture quotations, unless otherwise indicated, are from the KJV® and NIV®. Unless otherwise indicated. All Rights Reserved.

Printed in the United States of America

# Table of Contents

You are not Alone ............................................................. 1
Freedom and Truth ........................................................ 7
Start Speaking to your Mountain and See It Move . 13
A New Way to Think ..................................................... 19
Daily Portions ................................................................ 29
Overcoming .................................................................... 34
The View Has Changed ............................................... 41
Decree ............................................................................. 44
About the Author .......................................................... 46

# Foreword

In a vision, I saw a woman sitting on the floor with her hand reaching up. She did not think she could go on or that she was being heard. God revealed to me that this book is for her and many others who are feeling like they just need to be heard. If that is you reading this, remember that you are always heard and that you are "Never Alone." Leslie Tracey wrote this book with the love of our Father and the guidance of the Holy Spirit. I have personally seen Leslie go through an amazing transformation that can only be done by God. Embrace every word in this book and receive all the healing that is here. I trust that when you pick this book up, you will also be picked up from the places that held you captive. Accept the breakthrough of true healing that is being offered in each word. Let this book be the healing oil that pours over you as you receive the freedom that is waiting for you. As Leslie shares her heart with you, remember that she went from a place where all hope was hidden, then brought to a place where healing is freely given. God reached out and took her hand, just as he wants to do for you.

**-Barbara Rucci**
Co-Founder/Vice President, Double Portions Ministries

*Dedicated to my grandchildren*

*Riley and Avery*

*May you always hold the loving hand of Jesus as He guides you on your way*

"…. Yet I am not alone, for my Father is with me." ~John 16:31

Let these words be the very words of the Lord Jesus, spoken through me to you. How precious and loved you are, valued by Jesus himself. May the healing words spoken from the heavens be released and sent forth as a balm over your wound, a remedy to any situation where hope, light, and breakthrough is needed.

# **You are not Alone**

How I longed to see breakthrough in my life and situation that by all appearances seemed hopeless. Like a tunnel of winding darkness that had no end. The flame of longing quickly flickered out and I fell into a pit of despair as I watched someone I loved very much suffer a devastating physical trauma. As the circumstances progressed into a serious life changing situation, my despair grew. I had a deep longing to see the Lord reach down and miraculously save us all from this trauma, pain, and struggle of gigantic proportions. A longing to have the darkness recede, and be able to breathe freely again. Free of anxiety, worry, and dread of the future and all the potential it held for pain and despair. But as time went on, there appeared to be no divine intervention, at least not the divine intervention that I had envisioned on a daily basis. I slid down the slope of despair. The pit of hopelessness is where I landed and dwelled daily. My thoughts and actions were directed by the fog of depression and sadness that surrounded me. I stopped asking God for help.

I started asking the why questions. The all so common questions uttered in the midst of seemingly unfair situations. "Why God?" "Where are you, God?" These questions filled my mind, dictating my emotions and how I perceived my life. It felt like God had packed up and left and I gave those hopeless feelings a voice. I would say "God, why did you leave us?" or "God, where did you go?" The more I asked these questions, the worse I felt. Thankfully, today I have a better understanding. I now operate in a spirit of truth, rejecting strongholds of lies and thought processes built on doubt and unbelief. At the time of this crisis, I was too immersed in untruth to comprehend the magnitude of my questions. I was repeatedly asking the Lord a question that He had answered over two thousand years ago.

Perhaps you are in a very similar situation? Are your circumstances speaking to your emotions causing you to speak contradictions to the Word of God from your soul? Trauma can certainly bring us to a "faith crisis". Many questions present themselves in the time of our deepest struggle. This is some of my story and what I've come to believe and know through a power and name higher than any other name.

These are not simply words on a page, nor stories in a book. This is truth that is alive, active, and full of life. God is mighty to save and I have experienced His salvation first hand. I had all the head knowledge, but when the storm winds blew into my life, I did not have the revelation nor the power of the Holy Spirit behind the knowledge. It was through the trauma that I learned the love and security of the Lord and the power and reality of the Word. He is truth, and His promises are ever faithful. Hebrews 13:5 says, *"Never will I leave you; never will I forsake you."* In my despair, I had forgotten this truth.

All the dark questions I whispered in the hospital hallways and intensive care unit sounded so empty as the days and nights dragged on. With every bad report and bit of bad news my heart hurt even more. These drastic circumstances spoke to my emotions, saying, "God isn't in this." "Where are you God?" Standing in a church service one day while still in the middle of all the crisis, I sang along with the congregation a song that described Jesus as Messiah, Savior, and Healer. As I sang, Jesus Himself walked into the church. He stood in the row ahead of me. He was radiant light. Angels escorted Him on both sides. He stood right in front of me and spoke to my spirit. Spirit to spirit, my Lord said, "I never left you. See! It was like this", as he measured the very short distance between us with his hands. Then the Lord said "Look!" as He pointed to the left. There a calendar appeared. It flipped open. I heard, "All of your days". I could see all the days from the beginning of this crisis to the present day and then He said, "I was always there."

Then, the Lord touched my right shoulder and heat filled the right side of my body. I had needed healing in an area on that side and had not even thought to ask for it. Jesus took care of it though! Then, He turned with his angelic escorts and walked down the aisle to the other side of the church where I could sense Him being pulled by a family with a very big need. I learned several things that day. First, I learned that when we cry out to the Lord, He hears us and responds. Our deepest need draws the attention and presence of the Lord. The Word of God tells us, *"The Lord is close to the brokenhearted and saves those who are crushed in spirit"* ~Psalm 34:18. I experienced this myself as the Lord came to visit me that wonderful day. I also realized when he turned from me and walked towards the other family that it was our pain that attracted His very presence and love. His love came to deliver us, and His appearance proved it. The reality of Psalm 10:10 was mine. *"Those who know your name will trust in you, for you, Lord, have never forsaken those who seek you."*

He is truth, and His truth set me free from the lie I was bound by. I was never alone! Believing that lie plunged me into despair and depression, but the truth set me free. From that day on, I have known that I am not alone and I will never be alone. God did not leave me. He will never leave me, and He will never leave you. You are not alone. Your emotions and circumstances may be "telling" you you are, but the truth and revelation is, Jesus has never left you. When Jesus spoke to me in that church service and told me He had never left me, it wasn't just for me. It was for you also. I will speak over you now.

**YOU ARE NOT FORSAKEN.**
**YOU ARE NOT FORGOTTEN.**
**YOU ARE NOT ALONE.**

# **Freedom and Truth**

In the valley and darkest hour, you too can have your encounter with Christ. Have you professed or believed untruths or misconceptions? Perhaps you have been speaking them out of your mouth, over yourself, over your circumstances, or your life. Check your thoughts, check your words, and check your emotions. Are they lining up with the truth of God's Word? If not, cut them off now! Position yourself with the truth. Align yourself with the power of the Holy Spirit.

In order to receive freedom from the lies of the enemy, you must allow the undeniable power of the Holy Spirit to have full access to your mind. Ask Him to do a full and complete house cleaning. Get rid of all thoughts and beliefs that have attached themselves to you and your mind to keep you from the truth that Jesus is with you and will never leave or forsake you. Christ brings all the resurrection power of the cross into your life.

Where there has been death, Jesus brings life. The same power that brought Christ out of the grave is the power that lives in you. If you have confessed Christ as your Lord, Romans 8:11, *"And if the Spirit of Him who raised Jesus from the dead is living in you, he who raised Christ from the dead will also give life to your mortal bodies because of his Spirit who lives in you"* is your confession. Further on in that chapter, verse 12 says we have an obligation to live and be led by the Spirit. We have received a spirit of Sonship. Is this the context and position in which you live your life? Until my encounter with Jesus, who is all truth, I certainly didn't. John 14:6 says. *"'Jesus answered, I am the way and the truth and the life. No one comes to the Father except through me.'"*

Maybe Jesus will not appear to you in church as He did to me, but you can receive the ministry of Christ our healer in these very pages. For it is from my breakthrough to your breakthrough, from my healing to your healing. When Jesus spoke those words of life to me, it lifted me and broke darkness and despair from me. Today, take His words and His truth and apply it to your life right now. Allow the reality of my visitation of Christ to become your reality. Feel Him in your room, speaking the very words He spoke to me to you, Spirit to spirit. It is for you, your home, and for your family.

You are not or will you ever be separated from Christ. The power of our resurrected Lord lives inside of you. Dead things, dreams, relationships, losses, and finances can receive the resurrection power of Christ and live again. Speak this over yourself. These dry bones shall live according to Ezekiel 37:4 *"Then he said to me, prophesy to these bones and say to them,' dry bones hear the word of the Lord! This is what the Sovereign Lord says to these bones. I will make breath enter you, and you will come to life. I will attach tendons to you and make flesh come upon you and cover you with skin; I will put breath in you, and you will come to life. Then you will know that I am the Lord."*

The very breath of God is in you. You can use it to create life where the enemy has convinced you death is imminent. There is power in your words! Proverbs 18:21 says, *"The tongue has the power of life and death, and those who love it will eat its fruit."* Choose to speak life, declaring blessings and not curses. This is a choice you must make. God spoke the world into existence. He spoke the light into being in Genesis 1:3. He spoke the water and sky into existence in Genesis 1:9. In Genesis 1:26, He spoke man into being. The Word tells us that we are called to be imitators of God, therefore, as dearly loved children. ~Ephesians 5:1 If this is a mandate for us, why not start speaking words of life and truth into our own lives and the life of others?

In my time of struggle, I chose to confess lies and untruth. I spoke out of doubt and questioned if God was really for me. I wondered if I had been left alone to figure out my circumstances. The power of my words ushered in depression and hopelessness. The bible is a life source. Jesus has conquered death and the grave and has given us the keys to release life and heavenly resources over our needs and our loved one's needs. Matthew 16:19 says, *"I will give you the keys to the kingdom of heaven, whatever you bind on earth will be bound in heaven, and whatever you loose on earth will be loosed in heaven"*

There was a time in my life when I spoke from my unhealed soul. Out of my emotions, I spoke what I saw which were the "facts". Even as a mother, I felt it was my responsibility to spell out the "facts" and lay out what the future would hold for my child if he continued making bad decisions. I painted a bleak and dismal future for him with my words. One day, the Lord stopped me in the middle of a particularly bad episode of "fact telling". The Lord said "STOP!" That day the Holy Spirit took me on a journey of spiritual mouth washing in which He cleaned out my thinking, believing, and changed my speaking. This ultimately changed the behavior of my child and my family. If you tell someone they are going to fail, chances are, they will. Today, grab a hold of what the Holy Spirit is saying through me and let that be the meditation of your heart. *"The words of your mouth, and the meditation of your heart, let it be pleasing to the Lord"* ~Psalm 19:14.

# Start Speaking to your Mountain and See It Move

Are you cursing your circumstances by speaking facts (what you see and feel) rather than the truth (God's Word)? Curses come in all shapes and sizes. Speaking what you feel, and "spelling out" the facts as I did is choosing not to align yourself with the truth of God's Word, so curses will be the fruit of your lips.

Do you have a situation or circumstance that needs a turn around? The bible is a source of life. Start releasing the blessing of God's Word into that situation. Cancel all word curses that have been spoken and take hold of God's perspective. Release the very perspective of God through your words. Study the scriptures to fully comprehend what the Lord's opinion is, and make it your perspective as well.

Have you ever experienced a time when your mouth was moving faster than your brain? Your mouth firing off words so quickly that you realize you may have said something you shouldn't have. Have you experienced the conviction of the Holy Spirit regarding what is coming out of your mouth? Perhaps the words you spoke were harsh, rude, hurtful, or cutting. Or maybe your words simply did not line up with scripture. You need a spiritual mouth washing. 1 Thessalonians 5:1 says, *"Therefore encourage one another and build each other up, just as in fact you are doing."* The Holy Spirit is a wonderful spiritual mouth-washer. When you give Him access and permission, He can clean you up and get you congruent with the Word of God. Be sensitive to the moving of the Holy Spirit and allow Him to guide your tongue.

Are you in a place of desperation or maybe just ready to see a new thing spring forth in your life? A new thing like the one spoken about in the book of Isaiah. Take a moment to meditate on these scriptures and claim them as yours. Begin to decree them over yourself and your situation. *"Forget the former things, do not dwell on the past. See, I am making a way in the desert and streams in the wasteland."* ~Isaiah 43:18,19.

Unknowingly, I had created a wasteland because I didn't realize the power of my words. Not realizing the power of my tongue, I had spoken negatively over my family and environment and my words dried up my blessings. Each time I saw a situation unfold in my home, I spoke to it from a position of fear and uncertainty instead of a position of life and authority. With each unpleasant situation in my life, this vicious cycle of negativity and word curses repeated itself over and over again. I didn't know that my words had the power to create my reality as you can see in Job 22.28 (NASB). *"You will decree a thing and it will be established for you and light will shine on your ways"* Proverbs 18:20 says, *"From the fruit of his mouth a man's stomach is filled; with the harvest from his lips he is satisfied."*

The only remedy for this problem is to allow the Holy Spirit full control. Ask Him for a good picture of what His good plans are for you. He certainly has some good ones. Jeremiah 29:11 says, *"For I know the plans I have for you, declares the Lord, plans to prosper you and not to harm you, plans to give you hope and a future."* Ask the Holy Spirit what areas of His plans are you not in agreement with? What have you said or done to actually blow the blessings that God wants to give you? What has prevented the flow of the Spirit in your life? Take some time as I did and confess before the Lord your empty words. Confess the times you spoke contrary to the Word of God. When the Lord convicted me in this area, I stopped the behavior and spent quiet time before Him. I cried out to Him and repented for all the years of blindness to His Word and for the lifeless words I had spoken over myself and others. That is a spiritual mouthwash.

The next step I took was to seek the Lord for wisdom to speak life, blessings, and to speak alignment. To speak

His good will and His purpose for my life and the lives of those around me. I had to ask for wisdom because it didn't come naturally. "I was seeking God's way, no longer mine. I wanted His will to be done not my will. Just as Jesus taught us to pray in Matthew 6:10, *"Your kingdom come, your will be done on earth as it is in heaven."* The Word of God says if we ask for wisdom we WILL receive it! James 1:5 says, *"If any of you lacks wisdom, he should ask God, who gives generously to all without finding fault and it will be given to him."*

It was then that I really began a process of embracing the Word of God to discover what He had to say about everything. I started to seek Him in prayer for my children and my entire family. I wanted His will to be done and not mine, so I started seeking His way.

I took time each day to declare the Word of God over my home by taking certain key scriptures, particularly healing scriptures, and reading them out loud in each room of the house. I would also play scriptures continuously. At the same time, I began to speak with faith, calling things that were not as though they were according to Romans 4:27. Practicing this particular discipline was almost difficult at first because it was so opposite of what I had been doing for so long. Are you sick and tired of being sick and tired? Today is certainly a perfect day for a turnaround. Take the Holy Spirit's revelation to me and apply it to your own circumstances. You too can participate in your very own U-turn and see a dismal situation turn from despair to hopeful. Try it for yourself. Change your words and conversation and you WILL see breakthrough.

# A New Way to Think

When I began this new practice, it was a challenge not to speak from my natural man or from my emotions. But as time went on, the more I pressed into the Word and the Lord, the more I stepped into the flow of the Holy Spirit. Day by day, more and more life and truth came out of my mouth and poured over me and my family. What was happening? I was renewing my mind in Christ with the Word of God. As I grew in this process, I realized that I had built foundations in my mind. Some of those foundational beliefs were built on lies from the enemy that had become strongholds in my life. Some of the lies had been there for as long as I could remember, so it was normal for me and I was unaware that there was any other way to think or speak.

As the Holy Spirit was given full access to my life, these strongholds came down. My mind was washed with the truth of God's Word. No longer did I operate in the natural mind or out of my soul nature being controlled by my emotions. I became grounded and anchored with my feet planted on a firm foundation. The lies were uprooted and replaced by the foundational truth of God's holy Word. As the Word of God became active and full of life inside of me, it became a part of my regular vocabulary as well. It became a very natural thing for me to speak life and activate hope through the power of my tongue. Where there was once death, destruction, and despair, there was now abundance, restoration, and life by releasing the hope within. Renewing my mind was a process that began with yielding to the Spirit of the Lord, The Holy Spirit. I had to say goodbye to old patterns and generations of traditions, and grab hold of the very breath of the Spirit.

He will transform your life, your family, your home, your finances, and your relationships if you will simply let Him. Allow Him full reign, right now. Stop, pause, and render Him access to your situation. Allow the Lord to come in and take out the old. It wasn't working anyway. Allow Him to bring transformation, restoration, and rejuvenation; the glorious hope of a new life. One kick started by resurrection power and an almighty God! He can and will restore your mind. When He does, your relationships will change. He is that kind of God. He takes the old and gives new. He did that for me, and I know He will do the same for you.

Allowing the Lord to transform my mind and renew my spirit has given me beauty for ashes. The bible tells us in Isaiah 61:3, *"...to bestow on them a crown of beauty instead of ashes, the oil of gladness instead of mourning, and a garment of praise instead of a spirit of despair."* Where there had been death in relationships, I have now experienced restoration. The Holy Spirit has given me new life. Breakthrough after breakthrough. Transformation after transformation. I speak this over you, now. May my breakthrough be your breakthrough. From my house to your house, from my healing to your healing.

What I have discovered is when it seems like there are areas where I have "camped out" or felt a delay in a release from the Lord, there is a weakening of my faith. In the seemingly dark times when I was speaking to the darkness that had surrounded me, I had lost hope. This was an area in my life that was under the control and influence of a lie. I truly needed my mind renewed and washed with the Word of God! Every lie needed to be uprooted and exposed. I needed to come out of agreement with the dark thoughts that were clouding my judgement and protruding out of my mouth. If there was ever a time to agree with the Word of God and what the bible said about my situation, my future, and my children's future, it was then.

Replacing every lie with the truth took some time, but it was such a prosperous decision to break ties with destruction and agree with life. Our God is the author and creator of life (Genesis 5:1). Our God is a God that brings resurrection life for us. He is a God of power (Job 26:14). He is a good God who has good plans for your life (Jeremiah 29:11). This is the hope we believe. This is what we should agree with in our thoughts, words, and our actions towards ourselves and others.

Recently I heard the Lord say "I am the resurrection and the Life. Dreams WILL live again." There are dreams that have been lost due to illness and accidents and the Lord is resurrecting and breathing new life into those dead places. He says to you, "Check and see if there is not a stirring of the Spirit in a place of interest where all hope has been lost." The stirring is the Lord's breath of life, His resurrection power and dreams are being restored.

That is a good word, and we can all partner with the Lord and receive it. First, simply say "I receive." Then, make room for the miraculous by getting rid of old patterns. Those old patterns cannot support the weight of the outpouring the Holy Spirit wants to pour in. A new and fresh release is coming. It is strong and powerful, like a fire hose. The old pattern and thinking has got to go. You can receive your heavenly "all". You are making room for the miraculous.

Those old habits became crutches. Just as you would clean out a spare bedroom, throwing away junk, cleaning and applying a fresh coat of paint to the walls in anticipation for an honored guest's arrival, you must apply the same principle to yourself. In anticipation of the breakthrough God is bringing, rid yourself of toxic thinking and uproot lies by replacing them with the truth of God given dreams and the ability to carry out his plan for your life. We can cooperate with the creator of the universe and we can see the miraculous breakthrough in our homes. We are believing for breakthrough and by faith we are receiving it. Dry bones will live again. What are those dry bones? Lost relationships with those loved ones severed from you due to heartache, offense, circumstance, or loss in any area.

The Lord is restoring to His people and He is giving back generously. Take a moment now and receive Isaiah 61:7. *"Instead of their shame my people will receive a double portion, and instead of disgrace they will rejoice in their inheritance; and so they will inherit a double portion in their land, and everlasting joy will be theirs."* This is what God is doing now for His people. He is giving double for trouble! Blessings for curses. You can trade your disgrace for a double portion of the Lord's goodness. This is how He gives the beauty for ashes that the bible speaks about in Isaiah 61:3.

Let the Holy Spirit minister to you where you are right now, in this hour. This is your turning point. Receive the new work of the Holy Spirit. The old is gone, and out of the ashes rises a resurrected dream. Take it by faith! It is yours! With the key of David, walk through the door that opens because when it opens, no one can shut it (Revelations 3:7). It is the door to new life. Dreams restored! It is not a fairy tale. It is the almighty God singing over His people, a mighty warrior as Zephaniah 3:17 says, *"The Lord your God is with you, the Mighty Warrior saves. He will take great delight in you; in his love he will no longer rebuke you, but will rejoice over you with singing."* He takes great delight in you, rejoicing and singing over you. Breathing His glorious breath of resurrection DNA on your deepest needs. Restoration, hope, double portions, beauty for ashes, and joy. What a trade!

Today I hear the Father say to you "Hold your hands out and receive your portion for this day." Allow the Holy Spirit to pour into your uplifted hands a portion of what you need for today. What is that portion you need? Do you need joy? Peace? Breakthrough? Revelation? The Heavenly Father, who is the giver of all good things according to James 1:17, is offering you your daily portion for today. Just as Jesus prayed in

Matthew 6:9-11 *"Give us today our daily bread"*, your Heavenly Father is giving you the bread of life of Matthew 6:35. He is giving you Jesus Himself in life giving form. He manifests in hope, joy, peace, and love. He is your daily portion. He is your daily bread. Receive your portion for today by faith. Drink your portion for this day and say "I receive it by faith." For it is by faith that we receive. Hebrews 11 tells us what can be accomplished by faith. Jesus came so we could have abundant life (John 10:10).

What is your lack today? What area do you need an outpouring of abundance? What do you need a portion of in ample quantity? He is a God of plenty. King David said, "his cup runneth over." That is speaking of plenty and abundance. God is good and wants to restore and restock you. Do you feel your cupboards are bare and the supply is low? Reach out and receive! He is pouring your portion for today. Daily He gives us a portion. Jesus taught us to pray *"give us today our daily bread"* in Mathew 6:11. This could refer to spiritual food as well. Daily, you can receive from Him everything you need to persevere and overcome. Meditate each day on His Word. Take it as your daily nutrition.

There was a time and season in my life during prayer and meditation when the Holy Spirit would speak of daily bread and food from heaven. He would be specific for each day as to what was being released to me as far as provision and guidance. I believe this is for you as well. In the following pages you will find a week's supply of "daily portions". Read and meditate on each one, receiving for yourself what the Holy Spirit offers as your portion for today.

# Daily Portions

1. **Honey-** Ezekiel 20:6 *"On that day I swore to them that I would bring them out of Egypt into a land I had searched out for them, a land flowing with milk and honey, the most beautiful of all lands."*

   Receive the portion of the promised land, the hope for which you are called. Allow the Father to satisfy you with divine goodness. His kindness is better than life. He will pour something sweet out of a difficult and hard place. He makes all things new and provides honey from the rock. *"But you would be fed with the finest of wheat; with honey from the rock I would satisfy you."* ~Psalm 81:16

2. **Light-** Draw near to the undeniable source of light and power found in the Messiah's hands. Habakkuk 3:4 says, *"His splendor was like the sunrise: rays flashed from his hand, where his power was*

*hidden."* The power and precision lay in the hands of the Lord. Job 36:32 says, *"He fills his hands with lightning and commands it to strike its mark."* Grab a hold and experience the glory for yourself.

3. **Resurrection power-**. John 11:25 *"Jesus said to her, "I am the resurrection and the life. He who believes in me will live, even though he dies. And whoever lives and believes in me will never die. Do you believe this?"*

He is resurrection! Proclaim His name over lack, loss and illness. He gives back our dead. Hebrews 11:35 says, *"Women received back their dead, raised to life again."* Receive the reality of our resurrected Lord.

4. **Gemstones-** *Revelation 21:19-21. "The foundations of the city walls were decorated with every kind of precious stone. The first foundation was jasper, the second sapphire, the third*

*chalcedony, the fourth emerald, the fifth Sardonyx, the sixth carnelian, the seventh chrysolite, the eighth beryl, the ninth topaz, the tenth Chrysoprase, the eleventh jacinth, and the twelfth amethyst. The twelve gates were twelve pearls, each gate made of a single pearl. The great street of the city was of pure gold, like transparent glass."*

Receive your portion of heavens infrastructure. Let a part of heaven fashion you, shape you, form you, laying down a precious and ornate foundation in you. Heaven's glory is your DNA.

5. **Stew**- 2 Kings 4:38-41*"Elisha turned to Gilgal and there was a famine in that region. While the company of the prophets was meeting with him, he said to his servant, "Put on the large pot and cook some stew for these men. One of them went out into the fields to gather herbs and found a wild vine. He gathered some of its gourds and filled the fold of*

*his cloak. When he returned, he cut them up into the pot of stew, though no one knew what they were. The stew was poured out for them, but as they began to eat it, they cried out, "Man of God, there is death in the pot!' and they could not eat it. Elisha said, "Get some flour." He put it into the pot and said, "Serve it to the people to eat." And there was nothing harmful in the pot".*

Circumstances may have served you an inedible, poisonous meal as your portion. Perhaps you are being served bitter situations. The giver of all good things is pouring a remedy for you right now. The "flour in the pot" is the Lord's supernatural resources for you.

6. **Fresh Bread-** Exodus 25:30 *"Put the bread of the Presence on this table to be before me at all times."*

Always before the Lord, our offering is a fresh aroma to the King. Our lives are continually in the presence of the one true God.

7. **Towel**- John 13:4-5 *"So he got up from the meal, took off his outer clothing and wrapped a towel around his waist." After that, he poured water into a basin and began to wash his disciples' feet, drying them with the towel that was wrapped around him."*

The portion of humility and one on one attentive service and care Jesus has for each one He loves is here to clean you off and to minister to you. Behold Him as he is. The spotless Lamb of God, Savior of the world, and yet Humble Servant who cares about our most intimate needs.

# **Overcoming**

In the midst of it, it's hard to perceive or imagine anyone else's personal hardship being as bad as ours seems. As I sat next to my loved one's ICU hospital bed, watching the world go by through the window, I felt isolated and alone. By all appearances, all was well with the world. People seemed so happy and peaceful. Everyone seemed to have wonderful places to go to. Movies, dinner, vacations. Some seemed to be hurrying to pick up their children to begin enjoyable family time. My natural reality of being closed off from the world inside a small hospital room was also a picture of my spiritual state. Not only was I physically closed off, but I was spiritually isolated as well. I distanced myself from other believers that would be able to speak hope and life into me. I believed only what my eyes were seeing and my ears were hearing. There was very little truth being applied, as I was quickly adhering to fear and false beliefs. It would be several years before I was able to apply truth to those lies and begin to renew my mind from the strongholds the enemy had fed me.

Don't let this be you! You are an overcomer! We overcome by the blood of the lamb and the word of our testimony. *"They overcame him by the blood of the lamb and by the word of their testimony"* ~Revelation 12:11. When we truly partner with God and carry His vision for us, we overcome. We resonate with the ability to overcome on every level. Our spirit bears witness to what the Holy Spirit is saying as Jesus said Himself in John 16:33 *"I have told you these things, so that in me you may have peace. In this world you will have trouble, but take heart! I have overcome the world."*

Many of you feel alone and isolated today. Some of you feel betrayed. Situations and life circumstances have left others feeling that life is cruel and hard. Everyone has felt like life has been unfair at one time or another. There is a desperate need for the hope that is given through life in Jesus Christ. Let us lay down our heavy burdens and come to Jesus and find the strength and renewed peace that we, as well as the world we live in, needs. He is the ultimate giver. His resources never run dry. His mercy is new each day. His arms are outstretched to you. Nothing can keep you from Him. His love is stronger than any burden or shame you carry. Find Him, and you find the fountain of life. Many have traded their pain for His healing. They have received life eternal. His kingdom has come and His home is now their heart. The old made new.  He is a miracle worker in each one of us that have embraced His offer, *"come to me all who are weary and I will give you rest."* ~Matthew 11:28.

If you have struggled with pain handed down to you from generations before you, family issues, illness, or thought patterns, receive the Kingdom of God and all he offers. Be made new. Embrace the King of Kings, the One Who holds all the answers to your questions. The One who knows your future. Walk with Him. Make Him your Lord. Jesus is the way to eternal life. He is real love. When you encounter Him, you find your life will never be the same. If you have never had that experience, I offer you that opportunity now. Pray this simple prayer as a point of contact with Jesus.

*"Jesus, I am asking You now, come into my heart. Live Your life in me and through me. I repent of my sins and surrender myself totally and completely to You. By faith, I confess Jesus Christ as my new Lord and from this day forward, I dedicate my life to serving Him. In Jesus Name, Amen"*

This is not an "official" prayer of salvation, as there is no such prayer in the bible. This prayer is based on Romans 10:9-10 "that if you confess with your mouth, "Jesus is Lord, and believe in your heart that God raised him from the dead, you will be saved. For it is with your heart that you believe and are justified, and it is with your mouth that you confess and are saved." Praying this prayer in itself does not save you. Salvation comes from having a relationship with Jesus, but this is the moment in which you acknowledge His lordship in your life. This is the beginning of your walk with Him.

All these words have been offered to you. They have been collected through prayer, and written with you in mind. Structured and formed using the Word of God as the basis and backbone to present a message of hope to you. This book is a message for the one who feels left behind or forgotten, and the one who feels alone. These words have been seeds sown into your heart. But Jesus' words in the book of Mathew 13 :18 are a fresh reminder of what can happen to those seeds. He is speaking of the parable of the sower. Over and over I hear, "worries of this life and the deceitfulness of wealth choke it." Worry is a seed stealer. Jesus is showing us this in this parable. Not only can it steal the seed, but it can cause death to a place where there was once a vibrant healthy growth of faith. Don't let the worries of this life steal the seed of this good word that has just been planted in you. Let your life be good soil for God's Word to grow in.

As I meditate on the word today a prayer rises up inside of me. I release this prayer over you now. These are words formulated and shaped around the vitality and truth of the one true Word, the Holy scriptures.

*I pray understanding and the seed sown in you would remain in your heart. I pray your spiritual roots and identity would not remain on the surface. I pray that those roots would grow down into the depths of your heart and produce great perseverance. Like an anchor thrown into the sea on a ship, finding steady ground in a raging storm. Established, mature, and healthy roots grown and saturated in the word of God. I pray you will develop an ability to cast your cares on Him (1 Peter 5:7) for He cares for you. I pray the false illusion of wealth and the deception it can bring would not adhere to your heart. I pray that the fruit of the spirit is produced and will not be stolen! My prayer for you is one that Paul prayed for the Ephesian church. That the spirit of wisdom and revelation would rule in you. That the "eyes of your heart would be enlightened" that your heart would be the soil that prospers and grows large healthy crops in abundance with supernatural multiplication. The crops you produce would be a harvest of righteousness and peace. Proof that you endured the trials and tests. I pray the difficulties you have endured will be used as training. Instead of making you bitter, they will only make you better. I pray that out of the difficulties an endurance and growth will come forth, producing a tree of abundance in your life. May the tree of your life produce good fruit and resources for many to find strength in. But most of all I pray you persevere. I pray you remain hopeful, for those that hope in the Lord will NOT be disappointed (Isaiah 49:23)!*

# The View Has Changed

Today my view is on the other side of the street. I am looking across the street at a building I used to frequent. It is a therapist office. Many tears were shed on that side of the street. Between personal, marriage, and family therapy, I made 2-3 weekly visits there. I was in a constant search of a remedy for the never ending ache in my heart. After all the time I spent there, no solutions or hope was ever found.

Today the word I carry is one of a renewed hope. This day, I am brimming with expectation and hope brought on by the process of restoration. Healing has made its home in me. Jesus Christ my healer, redeemed me from the pit of despair and caused my feet to stand on firm ground. Oh, how my broken heart cried out for this so many years ago. I spent so many years sick and in pain. To be made new in my body seemed impossible. But then, I encountered Jesus and now I run with strength in my body, health in my bones, and my mind renewed. The spirit of heaviness is gone. I no longer struggle to find an answer or solution to my pain. I have been set free. I release that over you now. Be free. Be loosed from diseases, that grip onto your body. Let those shackles fall now. Let those chains that link you to your past be broken. Every entanglement and snare the enemy has used to bind you and keep you in a shattered state no longer exists. *"For whom the son sets free is free indeed."* ~John 8:36

Receive your freedom today. The anointing that breaks the yoke is here for you. The breaker anointing is the hammer that shatters the yoke of bondage. No shame, heartache, addiction, or disorder can prosper when the Holy Spirit tips the cup of renewal and healing to your lips. Drink deep and experience true breakthrough. Cross over to the other side of the street. The view is clear and bright and it is yours for the possessing. Just as the Israelites crossed over the Jordan into the promised land, out of slavery and into freedom. Just as

I crossed from one side of the street to the other from spiritual death to life, so I extend this offer to you. When we were young we were taught to cross the street holding hands. Today, there is a hand for you to hold as you cross your own street. Isaiah 53:4 says, *"But he was pierced for our transgressions, he was crushed for our iniquities; the punishment that brought us peace was upon him, and by his wounds we are healed."* Jesus has already paid the price for your healing, and He has the scars in His hands as evidence. He waits for you and wants to walk with you, crossing over to abundant life. I urge you to take His hand. Let Him lead you and you will find you will never be alone.

# Decree

Today I Decree That I am Not Alone

Today my Head rises off the floor

Today I am free from the anchors of sin that have held me down

I grab hold of God's hand, He is my refuge

His right hand upholds me

His gentleness makes me great

God has stretched forth his hand from on high

He has rescued me and delivered me out of great waters

I am strong and courageous

Fear cannot dwell in me

My thoughts are consumed by His Love

Anxiety is destroyed

Depression is no longer a stronghold

My feet have been set upon a rock
I am secure

I no longer carry an orphan spirit

I have broken through abandonment

I have risen over loneliness
Isolation can no longer hold me captive

There are new words in my mouth

God has come to me

I am a reflection of His Glory

Today, I receive divine power for in it is everything I need

His favor is pouring over me

I walk within God's love

His presence is my compass

I walk with His hand covering me

I NOW KNOW THAT I WILL NEVER BE ALONE

**~Barbara Rucci**

# About the Author

Leslie Tracey is co-founder and president of Double Portions Ministries. She is a speaker, teacher, mentor, and prophetic minister. Leslie co-authored a healing manual called *"How to be Made New"* with her ministry partner and friend Barbara Rucci. One of her greatest desires is to see hope restored to those who feel they have none. Leslie holds the words of Isaiah 61 in the core of her heart and ministry. She and her husband Walter reside in Illinois. They have three children and two grandchildren.

For information on how to:

- ❖ Invite Leslie to speak at your next conference, Bible Study, seminar, church, etc.
- ❖ To schedule a healing school or miracle service
- ❖ Learn more about Double Portion Ministries

Please visit www.dpministries.net

www.ingramcontent.com/pod-product-compliance
Lightning Source LLC
Chambersburg PA
CBHW072035060426
42449CB00010BA/2277